WAVING

TRACI O'DEA

ASSURE PRESS

Copyright © 2021 by Traci O'Dea

All rights reserved. No part of this book may be performed, recorded, used or reproduced in any manner whatsoever without the written consent of the author and the permission of the publisher except in the case of brief quotations embodied in critical articles and review.

An imprint of Assure Press Publishing & Consulting, LLC

www.assurepress.org

ASSURE PRESS

Publisher's Note: Assure Press books may be purchased for educational, business, or sales promotional use. For information please visit the website.

Waving/ Traci O'Dea— 1st ed.

Cover photo by Paul Hubbard
Author Photo by Erin Andrews

ISBN-13: 978-1-954573-02-4
eISBN-13: 978-1-954573-03-1
Library of Congress Control Number: 2021942151

ACKNOWLEDGMENTS

The poet gratefully acknowledges the publication of poems in this collection by the following esteemed journals, newspapers, magazines, anthologies, and institutions:

32 Poems
Barrelhouse
cellpoems
Ekphrasis
The Fiddlehead
Goethe-Institut
The Hopkins Review
The Jersey Evening Post
Literary Matters
Measure
Mezzo Cammin
Poetry
Poetry Daily
Queens' Quarterly
Unsplendid
Where I See the Sun: Contemporary Poetry of the Virgin Islands

The Albatross

Often, to entertain themselves, the crew would find
Some albatrosses, seabirds known for grace and force,
Those indolent companions who follow behind
The vessel gliding on its bitter, endless course.

As soon as they're abruptly dumped onto the planks,
These rulers of the blue, awkward and insecure,
Allow their vast white wings to piteously flank
Their sides and drag along the deck like useless oars.

Look at the winged explorer, so aberrant, weak!
Him, recently so handsome, who's now an ugly wimp!
One sailor puts his pipe up to the creature's beak;
Another mimes a flying cripple with a limp.

The poet is exactly like the prince of clouds
Who haunts the hurricanes and mocks the archers'
    strings;
Exiled to earth, surrounded by cacophonous crowds,
Her walking is impeded by her giant wings.

- CHARLES BAUDELAIRE

WAVING

The waves ignored the body, but it fought
        to shore against the tides that didn't know
     that they were what was keeping it from land.
  She stopped and watched it struggle, saw it caught
       inside the curl and swirl, the night-time show
         the sea puts on each evening with the sand.
All things wash up eventually, she thought
     and chose to take the road home, even though
        it passed the cemetery. Streetlights fanned
   colossal palm fronds at her feet that sought
  the farthest distance from the ebb and flow.
 And from her hair, her fingers pulled a strand
      of sea moss—flossy, taut—like ones that grow
        on seaside boulders, make them buffalo.

The most sought-after hand models look to have
    no bones. Just flawless skin
        with conch-pink palms,
            a wrist of wet, taupe clay on a potter's wheel.
           To be unnaturally natural.
             The money's in the muting.
               If anything but smooth appears,
                  it's airbrushed out. Just hold
              the shape, but don't remind us that it's there.
    No one wants to see the frame beneath.

Contrasting with Play-Doh purple fans
   of coral where they feed,
      flamingo tongue sea snails
         sport mantle skin of Pepto pink,
            with spots and yellow dots
               outlined in brown.
            The patterned skin glove shrivels with the snail
   at death, leaving behind plain white shell.

When I shook the poet's hand,
    her skin felt crinkly, loose
        like the vinyl tablecloth at Nana's house.
          Rippled from passing plates
             of goulash, beets, pineapple upside-down cake,
                picking crabs, from ballpoints signing checks,
            the crack and roll of hard-boiled Easter eggs.
         (When I made crayon art,
      the wavy texture transferred through
    the paper: grassy hills,
a house, sunbeams, a soldier's uniform.)
      The larger tears—repaired with masking tape.
         While others, fresh and small,
            were wide enough
               to wriggle tiny fingers in, extracting webs
                  of cotton insulation.
             Beneath her right hand's knuckled skin, I felt
        the dry, blank pages, words she never wrote.

The typing pool
in pencil skirts
stiletto overtop
the metal roof,
gather in gutter drains.
My cistern's full
of pantyhose and pearls.

At night I stagger breath to match the crash
(inhale), recede (exhale) of nearby waves.
I beg for their stampede to breach the road
and plow straight through my second-story door,
rush over me and pin me flat against
the bed with nothing but their pressure, weight.
Engravers, painters aim to capture them,
but I give in and let them capture me.
I know how futile replication is.
Courbet had to admit defeat, could not
come close to representing them, but what
he learned from his least still subject, he used
to make his deadest canvas come to life.

He made my scars
 look like an afterthought—
  flicks of his palette knife.
Mismatched nipples
 are swirls he pinkied on.
   They still look wet.
He didn't veil
   my scoliotic hips
  but stretched them out.
My map of veins
  is gone, but he applied
  the tint across my skin.

Two hundred thousand miles
    below the moon,
        the water splits
            over a rock and casts,
atop the blackwild sea
    towards the shore,
        an afghan, white—
            the kind my mom crocheted,
composed more of the space
    between the yarn
       than yarn itself.
          Its complex pattern snagged,
provided little warmth.
    I'd brush it off
       like salty residue
          from morning swims.
But Nana's blanket made
    from mismatched wool—
      her leftovers from
         other work—with squares
knit so tight light can't pass,
    I let enfold me like
       the flattest, calmest lake.
         We sold her empty house
and pier when I was nine.
    The pain that's coming
      tugs like undertow.

Turn out the lights. Let moths
live normal lives.
Days become nights—
flights, purposeless dives.

I.
The crystal jar atop the vanity
held hair that Nana gathered from her comb each day
after her hundred stokes. Once full, she'd stuff
a pincushion with the nest of grey. The oil
from her hair would grease the pins.

II.
In a drawer inside a jewelry box, I found,
along with fingernails and baby teeth,
the ribboned clipping of my first haircut
and touched the ends that sprouted from
my scalp inside my mother's womb.

III.
Before the chemotherapy, I made
you grow your hair then shave from head to toe:
armpits, eyebrows, pubic hair, and all,
so I could hold the strands of you I loved
that were already dead.

Five years ago today, I flew
                    across the hemisphere. Your blasted funeral.
It was supposed to be me. First,
                I smoke, no kids, divorced; I live
                        across the hemisphere. Blast it. Funerals
                        are just shit. I'm glad you're not here.
I smoke. "No kids." "Divorced…" (I live
                        to hear reports from our old friends.)
                    "…it's just shit." (I'm glad.) You're not here
                            to roll your eyes, give dirty looks,
                        sneer at reports from our old friends
                        whose lives, so meaningless, you gotta
                        roll your eyes. 'Don't give dirty looks
                            to me,' I want to yell at them.
My life: so meaningless. "You've got to
                        stop being dead, to switch places
                            with me," I yell. I went numb
                            five years ago. Today, I flew
                    to stop being dead. To switch places.
                            It was supposed to be me first.

Atop the dull, matte sand,
                      a glossy stripe,
silver, two inches long.
                      A lost barrette,
I think, or broken watch.
                      I see it flip—
a minnow.
        Caught in churning surf then dumped
with the white foam.
        Its gills quiver. Its jaw
unseals.
       I scoop it up to toss it back,
remember your last breath.
                      My hands on you.
Your head and skin
          almost as bald, streamlined
and deep-sea pale but luminous.
                            Your eyes
open but not on me,
                affixed instead
outside the walls. The way
                you froze when it
was done, your mouth agape.
                      Revived, the minnow
joins the shoal.

You're gone.
You're gone.
You're gone.
You're gone.
You're gone.
You're gone.

The starfish in the seagrass meadow seems
to have been made by Nerf—the puffiness
and symmetry, the red too red, the nubs
for grip. But it is real. Alive. Unlike
the thumb-sized star I thought, at eight,
I'd keep inside a sandy plastic cup
of ocean. As we rode three hours home,
I watched it fade from brown to tan to white—
its heart the last part to go colorless.
So I don't touch this vibrant one, just hope
it moves to prove it isn't fake. I'm tricked
by surface shadows, blades that jag and sway.
An arm lifts up, resettles, puffs the sand.
Each thought that's not of you—a victory.

No sand,
    but these soft stones don't hurt. The rough
        tide tumble made
                their edges round. I drop
    my sandals by a stylish group
                      of top-
      less moms and kids
          and turn off "tourist tough"
then shake my towel
            atop the rocks, sit down,
    peel off my dress,
                  exposing a giraffe-
  print two-piece number
          that I bought in town.
      I used my card
           to dodge exchange-rate math.
The act would change
          if she were here with me;
    it'd be a joke,
           like flashing for a beer,
or it would be a tease
             if you were here,
    more intimate.
           Instead, I can just be.

With eyes on the horizon line,
                    I reach
behind me, squeeze the clasp.
                        My back is bare
in a wink—then shoulders,
                    chest. No locals stare.
Two more misshapen spheres
                        along the beach.
A wave collapses on the shore;
                    a crack
of first contact then sizzle
                        through the stones
back to the sea,
            like blank cassette playback
or frying bacon fat.
                I call them stones
but half are sea-bleached skeletons—
                            grooved brain
coral, elkhorn, gorgonians.
                    I guess
how bright they once had been—
                        dressed to impress
stuck to one spot
            of undersea terrain.

I left Friday happy hour at nine p.m.
When I'd arrived, it hadn't snowed a flake.
Driving north, snow stuck like wads of phlegm
or wads of wet TP. I couldn't make
it home so thought I'd try your place. Stoned Jake
answered the door. I asked, "Is Parker here?"
then crashed with the cats till you nuzzled me awake.
Why wasn't there a storm like that this year?

"It's not a date," I told my mom before
you came around for Sunday night TV.
Mulder and Scully were locked behind some door
when my whole block lost electricity.
"It must be fate." You scooted next to me.
I groped upstairs to get another beer
and chugged it down while you got up to pee.
Why wasn't there a storm like that this year?

Your local bar was open, blizzard threat
or not. I smoked, drank pints, defeated you
at every pinball game, or you just let
me win. By the time we got kicked out at two,
the lot was white. I grabbed you by your blue
frayed hoody strings and pulled you in lest fear
could stop me. Minutes passed, then I withdrew.
Why wasn't there a storm like that this year?

June of 1816 saw a storm
dump snow throughout the Northern Hemisphere.
Folks stayed home and kept each other warm.
Why wasn't there a storm like that this year?

Verse One
It's more they fall for me
than I for them;
they're not my type,
or even my favorite archetype.
Drummers are the woodsmen,
marching us,
reluctant ones
to choruses of dwarves,
in Snow White's case,
or new, adoring parents in Corinth
for Oedipus,
saving us
from instigating oracles and glass.

Bridge
The orphan Dorothy's woodsman, tin,
had too much heart
but not enough for her.
That chopping robot wept rusty tears
only for himself.

Verse Two
Me, I'm a sucker for the forsaken,
an Oedipus
who needs Snow White
to slay with, not
a predictable woodsman
or a shepherd who can't
even kill when told. Don't get
me wrong, we are
indebted to the woodsmen,
our keepers,
they have their role,
but I'll take
the damned lead singer every time.

The harbor dock outside the restaurant
is shallow, less than three feet deep, and clear
with fields of minnows that I might mistake
for seagrass if I didn't know the sand
and coral floor are usually visible.
A stealthy tarpon causes the school to part
a perfect path, three inches on each side,
that closes up again behind him. Hunt,
he must, but I don't see him catch a thing.

"I won't wake up tomorrow just like that
and be in love with you," you say. Your eyes
and open-to-the-sternum cotton shirt
are the same blue. Your glasses, folded like
a crab and hanging from your neckline, pull
it low and tight against your sunburnt chest.

And then you say the thing you do to lure
me back. "Or I just might. You never know."
How you keep me around. But weeks from now,
you'll say it was my fault for having hope.
I leave the bait alone for once, until
the next time you let out a bit more string.

A shadow then a spear of pelican
dives in beside us, nets up minnows in
one graceful act. She surfaces—a splash,
then bobs and wobbles like a champagne cork.
Her veiny pouch aquiver, full of prey.

"We can get together, for these last
      few months," I say, "but there's no chance I'll move
           across the world with you, you know."
You know.
An expiration date.
      You find a job.
         I plan your Bon Voyage and help you pack.
But then you send a text: "I'd like to go
         to Anegada one last time before
            we leave."
You've accidentally written "we."
As if we are a we. As if we are
      both leaving here. Together. As if this
        is something that we want to save.

I let that "we" wash over me then sink
        into it, as I'll sink into, once you're gone,
         the almost-body-temperature September sea.

   Your bedroom's a cliché
from every movie made
   in these hot climes:
cathedral ceiling painted white
   with fans that spin at such slow speeds,
I ask you why
   you turn them on at all.
(You say they move like that
   from using so much force
to push the bloated air,
   like torque on an electric drill.)
Sahara dust
   coats spines of swollen paperbacks
that we've both read.
   The ready-to-be-boxed-up Christmas lights
are draped across a cranked-shut,
   louvred window which keeps out
mosquito bites. The gathered net
   is pulled aside, inert and grey.
The camera doesn't focus on
   the sweat that sticks our clothes to us
on sheets we've stained
   with ink, the springs that poke
against our ribs, or how
   the streetlight sparkles
on the rippled glass like snow.

My Jeep windshield's a piece of Plexiglas
that's so scratched up, I have to lean my head
outside, like a dog, to see at night. The gas
gauge and speedometer don't work. Instead,
I fill the tank from time to time and pray.
Pinprick-sized rust holes, inverted Braille,
let rain and sand sieve through the battered, gray
hot metal floor. The roof's a former sail.
But sitting in the split cloth seat, feet bare,
hair everywhere, as I steer on the high ridge
to town (moon peeping through palm trees to shine
on roofs, sea moss, and low-tide sand), the air
is like standing naked at the open fridge
deciding if I want water or wine.

"To have and hold until death do we part."
"To have and hold until death do we part."
They kiss and make their way down the narrow grass path.
Narrow and hold death down and kiss the grass.
We part their pathway until they have to make do.

"To the happy couple—a life without shadows."
"To the happy couple—a life without shadows."
Knives ring against glass to emboss their love.
Without love, a ring to glass.
Knives' shadows emboss the couple against their happy life.

"Love is a temple, love the higher law.
Love is a temple, love the higher law.[1]"
Over the floor they turn, spinning each other in circles.
Each law-spinning temple is the other.
The love-in circles a floor.

To love and to have love is love, in a way.
Happy to couple over the down floor,
without the other higher circles we make,
they hold their life-path—a ring spinning shadow's glass—
against the temple grass until knives emboss each narrow turn.
They do their part and kiss death, the law.

---

1. "One" by U2 from *Achtung Baby*

                    The dips and peaks inside the bowl—
                        flour, sugar, baking powder, salt—
look like quicksand
or cement for cement shoes.
                            Bam. I'm domestic.
                        This might as well be
a shopping list I'm writing.
(Though some can write a shopping list
                                        and make it ring like verse.)
                            A box of brown sugar, abandoned
        by a former tenant, is a brick.
I'll chisel off a chunk
                to give my loaf
                that certain sinful piquancy.
No yeast. Perfect.
My bread will be unleavened.
                    Wrong season,
                    but maybe they'll find
        some meaning
        besides ennui and sloth.
                    I use my Bic to shave some kumquats
                        because I'm out of lemons,
and this card calls for zest.
The recipe photo is unrecognizable.
                                I've substituted substitutes:
                        Jägermeister for vanilla
            for almond extract.
            I'm done.
                I push purée and pray.
                The oven's lit. It blazes like hell.

For one desperate week
                        she wanted you,
                                        to gnaw your cuticles until they bled,
then drain them dry,
                your bloods commingling. In bed,
                                she conjured up your eyes as green, not blue,
and pleased
        instead of pleading to undo
                              the spell she'd cast. Desire gave her head-
aches, stirred her ovaries,
                    made her hipbones spread,
                            her spine stack, her toes curl inside each shoe.
You never knew.
                But I did. So I pissed
                          a ring around you to keep her out, disinterred
the local vampire,
            asked when she'd been bitten,
                        wore the peacock pumps you couldn't resist,
crossed off each day,
            not worried or deterred,
                        reading her like a book that I had written.

                                In our town, peaks and valleys often switch,
          depending how the plates beneath us drift.
                                    I'll park my car uphill at night and find
it facing downhill the next morning. At times
                         smoggy sunsets are visible from our room,
other times the view's our neighbor's stoop.
                              Kaleidoscopic turns change right to left.
Streets start, hairpin, dead end, then start again.
                      No moss can grow: shade's never in the same
place long enough. It's our own fault, you say.
                     'Cause if we left, than we'd be more mixed up
without the shift and slip. We're better off stuck
                   in the game, letting the city roll us around.

                      In Scheeler's *Manchester*, the canvas weave
behind the paint shows through, gives blade to grass,
              stamps diamondplate on flat-stepped fire escapes.
The first dissolves into a building pink
                    as polished nails. The second ends a leap
away beside the second-story roof.
                      I jump to grab the bottom rung and miss.
Flip-flops become untoed; my skirt's askew.
                The next attempt—success. It slides down fast,
too fast, I think. I grab the paint-chipped rails,
            ascend to you. Each step springs up and down
like fun-house stairs. I feel aloft, weightless.
                  You're backlit at the top, a yellow glare
I willfully recall as being warm.

I wonder if I could form a pearl
      from the peanut nib my
            tonsil caught last night.
It doesn't hurt. My throat's an oyster
      swallowing sandy
           spinach I bought last night.
Before you died, you divvied up your things.
         For me, a watch
            & George's wooden teeth.
I usually disinfect them
      before I wear them out, but I
           forgot last night.
The words I can't write are the words
        I can't not write.
            Self-preservation censors me.
Genet did it, though. Unloved enough
      to spew the truth
           till his distraught last night.
As the cloud moved over us,
    I heard the hiss of raindrops
           displacing grains of sand.
The infinitesimal cacophonies
      camouflaged our shouts as
          we fought last night.
I trace mole trails in the yard,
    sink with each step, &
        squash their tunnels with my bare soles.
The sensation occupies me.
    I'll gladly think of anything
          that's not last night.

A wife sits on a bench in a solarium;
her husband stands behind the bench's spindled back

leans down on elbows like he would a jury box,
convincing twelve fine citizens the innocence

of the accused. She forces her eyes wide to feign
she's listening but stares beyond the sunroom's glass.

In contrast to her broom-straight spine and hat tied on
as if to lock her jaw, her arm—draped languidly

across the painted splat and staves that separate
the two of them—seems unnaturally relaxed,

at home, at ease. And in the center of Manet's
long-hidden masterpiece, her ungloved wedding hand,

the hand her husband's tapered finger and cigar—
like knives—are pointing to, rests limp, defeated, dead.

The painting's mostly green and blue with little red—
her lips, her cheek, and ear, pink blossoms just beside

her neck, one (rose? geranium? hibiscus?) bud
above her head, and one dark bloom behind his back.

We're sloths to hummingbirds,
so slow
they wonder how
we got from there to there.
Snails are simply rocks.
One afternoon,
I made you hitch
over the mountain
to admit a lie. When all
I really wanted was to lie
beside you on the beach
with elbows propped,
and fill in crossword squares
with one shared pen.
When race car drivers aren't at work,
they're forced
to share our roads.
To them, we're a traffic jam at 80 mph.
A traffic jam's reverse.
They advertise
themselves with iridescent plumes, kill
insects in midair,
hover to refuel.
Crashes scatter bits
of viridian and ruby smirched
with almost black.
My cousin mounts a piece of wreckage on her wall
and calls it art.

I. I wish we'd kept a trinket from our flat in Cannes:
   A. the pink ceramic teapot for our toothbrushes,
   B. a broken shutter slat,
   C. a sprig of money tree.

II. I unintentionally brought back some air.
    The spring after you left, I opened up a vacuumed bag. The scents of sea, stale wine, macadam filtered through my unpacked clothes in Baltimore. In fact, it wasn't air, but missing air I'd pressed and emptied out, an underscent we never registered. It didn't smell like anything but what I wasn't breathing here.

III. I'll probably resort to power tools.
   A. I want to drill a hole into my heart
      lobotomize the spot once filled by you.
      My right hand could keep writing while my left
      hand cleanly bored a hole so thin that when
      the spinning sliver was removed, it'd heal
      like Wolverine or Jell-O cubes.
   B. While chopping onions with my newest knife,
      I sliced clean through the web of skin between
      my thumb and index finger. Frightening
      to see a wedge cut from that taut unbroken arch.
   C. I rinsed and sealed it right away and bound
      the digits for a week. The cells rejoined,
      repaired themselves, and now the scar
      has made that spot a little stronger.

No more walks in the 'hood.
      Construction fence keeps me
          from standing near the place
where I first rose and stood.
      The rowhome where I was raised
         is razed, a parking lot.
No more walks in the 'hood.
      The alley where we shot
         hours and hours of hoops
is ground with all the stoops
      where our moms would chase
         their gin with beer in crazed
teacups. I'll never be
      the girl next door to you,
         the girl next door. It's good
we didn't have the view
      of bulldozers passing through
         the common wall where we tapped
Morse code. It's dust now, scrapped
      with lies of how we would.
No more walks in the 'hood.

When she stays here with me,
     I make her feel at home,
indulge her taste for floral prints
      and accent pillows, drapes and bedding sets
offset by rugs of yellow, violet, green.
     But when she heads back
to those scuffed and marble hallways that construct
      her life away from me,
I pack her frilly things, revert to minimalist hues
      of blank white tarps, bare windows, empty canvasses,
and sculpted trees with limbs that reach for Zen,
     not Zeus. It's when she's gone that I'm at home.

I'm giving them away.
Today, my words are free,
as in, no charge to you, nor any cost to me.

What's changed is that I know they're lies.
It's nothing new;
the same old words I used before but called them true.

Last year, I could've sold you insight by the pound—
some sage advice or rule I'd traded for or found.

It's not false advertising if I bought it, too.
The boldest lie I sell myself? That there's a you.

It's like the genius who
pursues
the final decimal of π:

the more she calculates
and marks
down yet another numeral,

the further she becomes.
When all
she has to do is simply look

at any circle to
observe
the truth of what's in front of her.

Against the frame,
arms crossed, she watched
another bumbling locksmith
try his best.
This one fumbled
but with confidence.
When it unlatched,
she stared at him,
impressed.
She then mistook the light
reflected in his eyes
for something that
originated there
(like one pretends
the moon's cold warmth
comes from the rock itself).
The radiance that shined
on her through him
was what she sought, she thought.
Flattered at first,
he held her gaze and smiled,
but then he humbly bowed
and took his leave.
She pivoted and faced the source,
the open door.

         Rimbaud pressed his palms
against his eyelids, hard.
         Among the tessellated spheres,
he saw a hybrid beast:
                  a lion, scorpion, and owl
(and its eye was its heart,
                  and its heart was its eye).

I've never claimed
        to need them for support;
                their job's to make
                        unseemly bulges smooth.
                              Each has its own appeal:
                                  long ones, short
                        ones, French, Italian style.
                  I try to soothe
            my inner feminist
      and say I'm more
than feminine in traps
    designed by men—
          they hide a bit
                of padding and restore
                        my form to its former self.
                          Oxygen is overrated,
              anyway. I need
          less space to breathe
        than most. I find I'm out
    of sorts when not contained;
I'm far from freed.
    I'm not the first one
        to believe, no doubt,
            that liberation means
                that anything
                    can fit with just a bit
              of shimmying.

I don't know what driftwood should
				look like. Uncut, I guess, but smooth.
This piece was once
				a baseball bat before it struck home, tossed
in pride from some cruise ship
				back when the decks
had sodded stadiums and stands to lure
				son-centered families aboard. I hold
it in my hitting hand.
			The weight's too light
for leather-covered regulation balls
				but perfect for the fallen almond fruit I pitch.
I lob one out to sea and hate
			admitting that whenever I perform
some act I typically align
			with them,
I make believe I have an audience.

To comfort her,
          they say that getting raped again
                    would be like getting struck by lightning twice.
          A lie.
How could they mention that
          statistics prove that once
                    you're raped, you're like a broken foot?
          The cast is off;
the doctor says you're good
          as new, but two years down
                    the road, you misstep and fracture it again.
          This time,
the warnings come:
          how maybe you should "watch your step"
                    and now it's prone to injury,
          but it's your foot,
and you're not wearing
          orthopedic shoes, so next
                    time at an outdoor concert when
          some frat boy comes
down right on top of it,
          you don't even waste your time
                    with the ER. Instead, you go home
          and have a soak,
stay off your feet,
          then wrap it tight for a week or so
                    until it doesn't hurt too much to walk in heels.

Cast off, her legs are asymmetrical.
They don't appear to be from the same girl.

The fractured right is fat around the knee
but wasted, dented in above the thigh

like it's been struck. Left tapers as it should.
And though she shaved them both this morning, Right

is dotted prickly black while Left feels smooth.
Right foot's edemaed, scarred, and bruised. When not

concealed, it sunburns easier than Left.
Both limbs are cursed or blessed, she isn't sure,

with veins beneath the skin in cinder grey
that seem stagnate but hide the gush inside.

They trace lines to her heart like termite trails
ascend to bulbous nests on sea grape trees.

I wouldn't call the green
                      a poison green—
it's several shades removed
                    from Mr. Yuk,
and over that's
             a less-than-shiny sheen;
the way unpolished
               mangoes often look.
I waved away the warning signs
                         —the clutched
snakeskin around
               a lower branch, the fact
that not one fallen apple
                   had been touched
by birds who should've called
                        the fruit their snack.
The taste surprised;
             no bite like you'd expect
from sour Day-Glo treats.
                 Instead a spurt
of liquid that had ripened
                 to collect
flavors surrounding it—
                sunbeams, the surf—
and turn them into crème
               brulée. My breath
and lips soon burned.
              I knew I'd savor death.

           My driveway floods,
the propane tank becomes
                dislodged,
resulting in a maple smell
                  in my apartment—
leaking gas.
     The first time it occurred,
I spent the night downstairs
                in a spare flat.
The second time,
         I wedged the doors
and windows open, less afraid
                    of bugs that might creep in.
Then after that,
        the screens only.
I ached the whole next day.
                Last night I woke up cold
and closed them all,
          turned off the fan.
The head-inside-the-oven-trick
                has always seemed
absurd to me,
     some self-inflicted
gingerbread-house end.
              Why be the witch?
I woke this morning
          disenchanted,
like all sleeping princesses.

Seaspray dots the foredeck glass.
A blob of water twitches,
jigs its way toward
the metal center seam
to join the stream
that pours into the sea.
It sometimes seems
to change direction
for a second,
tries to force its heft,
or volume, back to stay
as this amoebic droplet
that exists
as surface tension,
nothing more.
But that's enough.
To be a mass against the glass.
In dreams, I try to splice
my fingers to
chain-link fence,
or bolt them onto it
with locks whose wishful keys
litter the Seine
from paramours who split
decades ago.
So when the last tsunami comes,
I will remain up here,
buoyant and parallel
to temporary sea bed,
ocean floor
that now is simply ground
I'm walking on.
I'd rather lurk
in dirty, murky jade—
a most unnatural shade
composed of silt,
Coke cans, tree branches,
rusty bottle caps,
than be sucked out to depths
that crush but sell
themselves in rainbows, pink
and purple hues
as innocent as children's cereal.

The summer garden's growing weeds,
obscene zucchinis, and tomatoes spilling seeds.

A month has passed since I last walked the rows
where only that which wants to spoil grows.

Hoping to discover something sweet,
I search among the overripe and torn. Between my feet,

a watermelon sits,
small as a bocce ball. Mismatched markings trick my eye; I think that it's

been squashed or cracked,
but passed between my palms, it's warm, intact.

I bet it can't be edible, but something makes me wonder what I'll find
inside: some weevils, powder, solid rind.

I grab the melon, leave
the rest to rot. It rolls toward the sink before I cleave

the ball in half. The core is organ red. I've lost
the bet. I scrape some off the top like frost

across a windscreen, only it's not cold
and tastes like molten honey, gold.

Earthworms trail illegible,
                zigzagged script
                              across a wash of sand that's overflowed
the corner of a sidewalk square—their last
                living mark
                      before they bake aboveground.

The final message is left
                in death itself,
                      a solitary character on concrete:
an S, a P, a J,
        or a letter coined
                in alphabets that I was never taught.

The corpses harden
            and decay, or when
                    still wet are lifted up by soles of shoes,
or stuck to tire treads,
            leaving behind
                        an untranslatable stain of skin and guts.

Weaving between them,
            I wonder which way's up,
                      if a Z's really an N, wanting to dig
beneath the earth
            for their Rosetta stone,
                reveal the reason behind their flaked remains.

Body bags undertake
            the opposite route,
                straightened from their fallen, crumpled shapes,
dragged across the sand.
              Their final mark
                    is hidden once they're settled underground.

Each time I try to write my head,
I end up writing feet instead.

The thing I fear the most
for them? The words.
Language misleads.
It disconnects
them from the frequency
so close to them.
In them. On them. Of them.
What can't be said.

Flat words aren't close enough.

They leaden down the levity,
the opposite of alchemy
(like Robert Bly has said
of fact-filled verse:
"poems are heavy...
solid like a toad
which has eaten
ball bearings.")

They weigh.

ABOUT THE AUTHOR

Born in Baltimore, Maryland, Traci O'Dea is a writer and editor currently living in the Channel Islands, UK. She has an MA and an MFA from Johns Hopkins University. Her book, *Restricted Movement* (Scotland Street Press 2021), includes paintings by her father. Additionally, her work appears in *Poetry, Poetry Daily, Literary Matters, 32 Poems, The Jersey Evening Post, The Fiddlehead, Where I See the Sun: Contemporary Poetry in the Virgin Islands,* and elsewhere.

www.traciodea.com

linkedin.com/in/traciodea
youtube.com/TraciODea
instagram.com/traciodea

www.ingramcontent.com/pod-product-compliance
Lightning Source LLC
Chambersburg PA
CBHW021452070526
44577CB00002B/371